To Ventureet

life is a journey and this is mine.
I pray as you love & live that your
journey honors him in all you do

God Bless
Craig Horne

The White Afrikan

~Who became an
African-American~

Table of Contents

Table of Contents

Protection for the White African

My story begins in South Africa where I, a white man, was born and raised. There was change taking place in the country back then, a change in the feel of the land in the early 80s. When I ponder those days, I remember how wild my upbringing was. I think about how many times I was in dangerous situations, either alone or with friends. There were also times I helped others out of dangerous situations. Looking back, it appears danger was a theme that ran through my childhood and teenage years. As an African-American now with a very different life, it's interesting to see how I was molded and changed by those experiences.

My life can really be broken into several small segments that shaped my perspective of life and who I am today: growing up in South Africa, my move to America, life as a young man, marrying my wife, and moving into ministry. As God has moved me from place to place, I've seen Him do some amazing things. I've also seen some dark and difficult times. But one thing is clear as I look back across the years, God always had His hand on me. As a friend, a husband, a father, a pastor, and even as a child, God was there and He was guiding me.

In this book, there are some wild and crazy stories, and some fun and interesting stories. The tricky part has been knowing which ones to include. There are just so many! But I hope you will see through the chapters of my life that God has been moving me all along into the man He has called me to be.

Things have been revealed to me along the way, in different parts of the world, through different people. I hope to express my gratitude to all of them who have been part of my journey. And I offer this narrative to my kids, who will one day share it with their kids...the life and times of the white African, the African-American man, and the power of God.

The White Afrikan ~Who became an African-American~

A Champion Dad

M y dad grew up poor in a tough and difficult environment. His dad worked two-three jobs just to put food on the table. He had one pair of school clothes that were washed each day and holes in his shoes. The kids would make fun of him because he lived in the very poor part of town. He would fight for his honor most days and became known as a tough guy, someone you didn't mess with. This reputation would eventually follow him to school. Really, I think the pain from the premature death of his sister to pneumonia stayed deep in his core and created a resistance to God but also helped make him who he was.

My grandfather would routinely beat my dad for various reasons with his belt. He seldom spoke to him, and he never once told him he loved him. He would just sit in his chair and gaze into the room for days on end without uttering a single word to his wife and son. In fact, the only regular contact between my dad and his were the spankings. He would often choose to misbehave just to get his father's attention. My father swore if he ever had kids, he would teach us two things: one, that he would always love us and make this known to us, and two, to always forgive. Despite his upbringing, my father was loving, fun, and spontaneous, a firm but fair man, and I have many memories of him.

I remember when I was young, if my dad had been away on a trip, we'd come home to find a chocolate hidden under our pillows. It didn't happen often, but he would do it just to remind us that he'd thought of us.

After work each day, my dad would ask my mum the same question, "Did Craig behave himself?" My mum would say, "Nope, he misbehaved." That was normally the answer. I was not mischievous, I was just full of energy, but I would often get into trouble. My dad would then tell me to go to my room where I had to wait for him. The conversation that followed went like this:

Dad: "Do you know that you've misbehaved today?"

Me: "Yes."

Dad: "Do you know that it's disrespectful to behave that way to your mum?"

Me: "Yes."

Dad: "Do you know that I love you?"

Me: "Yes."

Dad: "Well then, I have to spank you."

He would spank me two or three times with a cricket bat, and after, as I was crying, he would look at me and say, "I love you. Give me a kiss." I would kiss him, and he would say, "You come out of your room when you're ready to play." When I left my room, all was forgiven, there were big hugs waiting, and I would either go play an indoor soccer match in the lounge (where we would break most of mum's favorite things and then superglue them back together), or go outside and play a game of cricket or baseball, or swim in the pool.

Every night before I went to bed, my father would wrestle with me. As he approached my room, he would stomp his feet and yell "Boom, boom, boom!" in a manner reminiscent of the theme song from the 1986 movie about Shaka Zulu, the famous warrior king from our town. My father would clap and mimic this thunderous music as his war cry as he came toward me. After we wrestled, he'd say goodnight and pray for me. Then he'd say, "You know you're a champ, right?" and I would say yes. "And you're not only a champ, you're a champion." I heard that word over and over again.

Dad always had time for me. He had been a great athlete and spent a lot of his time off helping me and coaching me when I was younger even though I didn't listen much. He would always encourage me, but keep me humble at the same time. When I got older and had a great game, he would ask if there was anything I could have done better, any parts of the game where I hadn't given my best. And when I'd had a poor game, he would point out to me the moments or situation where I'd played really well. "Remember those," he'd say. He always tried to keep me grounded.

Whenever he dropped me off at school, he would say the phrase "Do your best, forget the rest." This was a very powerful statement growing up. The best was asked of me, and my best was whatever I could do. He never got upset with my grades if I did my best in studying. I wasn't a great student, but as long as I was honest about whether or not I'd given my best, that was okay. We wouldn't have a major conversation about it.

He was a very strong man, mentally and physically, not scared of anyone or anything. I think he kept a lot in about his youth. I think there were many things he did that he couldn't speak about and was maybe even ashamed of. I only saw him cry once. This doesn't mean he wasn't affectionate, because he was always hugging and kissing me and wrestling with me, but there was a part of him that was hard. The one time he cried was when his father-in-law, his role model, passed away. My dad was supposed to speak at his funeral, but he struggled to get the words out through his tears. That's the first and only time I saw him cry. In fact, when I left for America on a soccer scholarship, he was the only one in the room not crying. He simply said to me as I boarded the plane, "Son, you've made me proud. Continue to." My mum called me the next day and said, "Hey, Craigy (which is what my dad used to call me), I know Dad didn't cry at the airport, but when he came home, he took your rugby jersey, tied it to the bed, and sobbed all night."

Looking back, I believe I was my dad's champion. I believe that I honored him in the things I said and did. I didn't get everything right, and neither did he, but he was the greatest role model I've had in my life. My father was a strong, hard, kind, funny, spontaneous man of God. He taught me to love others and love myself, but more importantly, he taught me to live as a man of God, a man of faith. Who he is and how he raised me changed the trajectory of my life. Without his guidance, I could have gone down a different road, the one many of my friends took who had similar fathers. This would have derailed me. I believe that my relationships are influenced for the better because of my father. Dad, you're the champ.

The picture my dad drew for me when I left home. It hangs on my office wall now to remind me where I'm from and who I am, an African warrior.

A Mum who Loved

My mum was always kind and generous to me as I was growing up. I can remember, even from a young age, that my sisters thought I was the golden child because mum always looked after me. Maybe, in the beginning, they thought I was a mommy's boy, before dad took over and began making me a man.

I remember being hugged and kissed often, a continuous stream of love shown to me. On a regular basis, when she picked me up from school, we would go down to a local mall before going home and we'd do some shopping. She would look through some clothing stores, pick up some medication for my sister, Shelly, do a little grocery shopping, that kind of thing. She would always buy me a little treat, a little something, maybe a bag of french fries from Wimpy. If I was lucky, it might be a hamburger or a small chocolate. If we drove past a tea room, we'd get a pie. Yeah, I remember those days very, very well.

My mum would always be inviting my friends over. They'd come over and destroy the house and she never once moaned about something being broken or the noise level. She gave me freedom in my own house to have fun, be a boy, and later, a man.

I have such good and fun memories. I remember being lazy at times in the mornings, knowing that in a few minutes my dad would walk by and make sure I was out of bed. When I wasn't, mum would put my socks on while I was sleeping, and then grab me and get me out of bed before dad came to check on me. And she taught me how to treat women and how men should be treated by women.

My mum was always looking out for me, wanting only the best for me. She was my biggest supporter in all my sports, confirming to me that I was the champion my dad said I was. She was an encourager and showed only kindness and generosity toward me. She praised me, reminding me who I was, a child of God. I am very thankful for a mum who spent many hours loving on me and preparing me for my wife. She is a gift from God. Thanks, mum.

My mum speaking life over my son when he was baptized in the same church as my grandfather, my dad, and me

The White Afrikan ~Who became an African-American~

How Grandparents Leave Legacy

I was very fortunate to have both sets of my grandparents up until I was in my early 20s. On my mum's side it was Grandpa and Granny Mac, Donald and Eunice. They were very kind and accommodating grandparents. We would often go up to their house in December to celebrate Christmas together. They lived in Pretoria, South Africa, for most of my life.

Grandpa Mac was a famous preacher. He was the president of the Baptist Union. He oversaw all the Baptist churches in South Africa. He had a great message. He was a preacher, known for his teaching and good character. He was a man of prayer and wisdom. He was one of the main reasons my dad gave his life to Christ and followed God. That decision changed my dad's life, and obviously, mine, and my family's. Grandpa Mac's wife, Eunice, was a kind, helpful, and caring lady who fully supported her husband. Towards the end of my teenage years, they moved to Durban, South Africa, and ran the local church there. This is where I lived.

Our family would often go to their house for lunches and dinners and he regularly came to watch my games. When I was struggling with Afrikaans in school, my second language, he stepped in and helped me and got me through that. He was a great man of God, a great role model. Grandpa Mac was someone who changed many lives because of his example.

On the other side, we had Granny and Grandpa Horne, Connie and Allen. Allen was a hard man and a veteran of World War II. When he returned from the war, he went through a period of depression. The war had broken him a bit, and he did not know how to manage himself. He was tough, as hard as nails. He treated my dad tough too, when he was young. Like I said before, Grandpa Allen never once told my dad he loved him. Despite this, he was a good, hard-working man who provided for his family.

Connie, his wife, was the kindest woman I've ever met. She was a great cook, and very hospitable. She'd give you whatever she had. They lived in the same town as me, and every Sunday, I would go there for Sunday lunch, a home-cooked meal of meat, potato, veggie, dessert, and a soda. I spent many hours there each Sunday playing chess with my grandpa. I beat him once, but he denied it. We had many conversations about life. One of my favorite sayings from him is, "Don't accept wooden nickels." I kind of carried that through my life.

My granny died of cancer. Actually, all of my grandparents did. And that's when I saw my Grandpa Horne change a bit. His heart softened and he connected with his son, my father. They had a great relationship in his last few years. He became a Christ-follower and man of God. He was baptized when he was in his 80s, just to prove that he had changed his life. It meant a lot to me that my grandparents were invested in our lives. Both sets of grandparents loved God but expressed that love differently. By the time I left South Africa to go to America, I had received a full measure of my grandparents' love and teaching, and it served me well. When I returned four years later, they would all be gone. My kids would never get to see their great-grandparents, but they would treasure their gold.

Grandpa Mac, Granny Mac, Granny Horne, and Grandpa Horne

The White Afrikan ~Who became an African-American~

That Dam Wall

———◆◇◆———

We didn't get to go on many vacations in South Africa, but every once in a while my father would surprise us. One year we went to an amazing place called Spioenkop Dam Nature Reserve, an almost 11,000-acre savannah full of wildlife. We were going on safari.

We stayed in a rondavel, which was like a hut, made our own food, and enjoyed our time at the dam, which was like a reservoir only bigger. The entrance to it was fenced in to protect us from the animals, where we could swim and play.

Six of us went out on a sailboat one day, my uncle Gary who is a 6-foot plus, strong, wild-looking man, another uncle, DJ, my father, me, my sister, and our cousin, Lorryn who was five. We were having a great time flying around on the boat.

Uncle Gary took the wheel, and being the crazy man he is, decided to head toward the dam wall, which is where they release the water when it gets too full. As we got closer to it, everybody told him to chill out and slow down and steer away from it. But he decided that he would get as close as possible to the buoys that prevent you from getting too close to the wall. He was headed straight for them and moving fast. At the last minute, he turned the boat. But what he didn't know is that in the process, he'd snapped off the rudder.

The boat capsized and we all fell in. We were scattered in the water, sputtering, and trying to breathe. The only one who had a life jacket was Lorryn. My sister grabbed her. Everyone else was treading water trying to stay alive.

Gary pushed the boat back over. He got on one side with my sister and cousin, and was able to balance the boat by moving to the upper side of the broken rudder. They slowly made their way back to shore in a zigzag pattern. My other uncle, and me and my dad used the ropes from the buoys that were separating us from the wall to make our way across to the side of the dam. Praise the Lord they didn't open the dam wall at that moment.

As we looked at where we were and where we needed to go, we realized it would take six or seven hours at least to get there. I was 12 years old at the time, and my dad said, "Come on, you're a big man. Make it happen." We walked and walked and walked. Several times he told me to stop. We'd stop, hang out for a little bit (maybe 10-20 minutes), and sometimes sit or lie down. Then, we'd get up and walk. I didn't know why we kept doing this. Our hope was that the rangers would find us on the dam south of the wall, and they'd pick us up and drive us back to our camp. At one point as we were stumbling down the path, we heard a loud noise from some wild animals. It was kind of scary. About five minutes before we would have made it back to camp, we were picked up by the rangers and taken back to our family.

That day I walked for many hours. When we got back to the camp I asked my dad, "Why did we sit? Why did we lie down?" Come to find out, many of the animals in the safari were drinking from the dam while we were walking. It was for our protection that we stopped and hid. That dam wall had nearly killed me.

The White Afrikan ~Who became an African-American~

The Ride of My Life

———◆◇◆———

It was a summer's day in Durban, South Africa, and we were off to Water World, a massive water park that we used to attend when we had the money. This park was known for its wild and crazy rides. On some of the rides, people would get knocked out or lose teeth. There had even been a few deaths on the ones that were outrageously out of control. I was 14 years old and with my mates and we were looking to be equally wild and crazy.

The day started off great with friends racing each other on every ride we could. One of our favorite rides was an enormous concrete wall that was like a slide, probably about 30 feet high top to bottom. When the ride was first introduced, they had you ride on your bum, but too many people were injured that way, so they added inner tubes to each lane. Of course, what happened then is that people would race each other all the way down. The one who got to the end of the pool first was the winner.

The White Afrikan ~Who became an African-American~

The weather was hot, the competition even hotter. Between me and my friends, a champion would be named that day. This is how it went: find your tube, lie down, wait for the lifeguard's whistle, and then, you were off! You would fly down on your inner tube, with just a thin layer of water between you and the concrete slide, picking up speed as you went, going over a few bumps, and then hitting the water and bouncing to the end of the pool.

After coming in second a few times, my uncle Gary came to me and said, "Hey, I think you can be the champ. I know how to win." He continued. "I'm gonna jump on the tube, kneeling," (which is illegal), "And then you jump on my back," (also illegal), "And because of our weight on this tube, we will slide down and beat everybody." Knowing the lifeguards would not be happy about this, we had to act fast. "Don't wait," he instructed, "As soon as I get on my knees, run and jump on my back, and we'll be off."

The plan was set. I was in second place, wanting to be in first. My mate got on his inner tube. My uncle said, "Hey, I'll race you," and he jumped on his inner tube on his knees. Immediately, the lifeguard blew his whistle to stop, but I ran, jumped on his back, and the race was on. Straightaway we took the lead, flying with major speed. We hit the first bump, got a little bit of air time, hit the second bump, increased our air time, and by the time we hit the third bump, we were in full flight - at maximum speed. We could not even see my buddies behind us. They were left in the dust, or more accurately, the spray. As we started getting close to the water at the end of the ride, I realized we were going way too fast. There was going to be a massive wipe out, no two ways about it. We hit the water with such a force that I flew off my uncle's back and went straight in, down to the bottom of the pool cracking my head on the floor. When I came up out of the water, I had split my chin. Blood was pouring out and I was really dizzy. I didn't know where I was. And all my uncle said was, "Forget the blood, you may even have gotten knocked out, but you're the champ."

They closed down the ride for the rest of the day, but yeah, I was the champ, and I have a major scar on my chin to prove it. That was definitely the ride of my life and my uncle was my nemesis once again.

The White Afrikan ~Who became an African-American~

Becoming Dog Food

The actual dogs that attacked my uncle

Me and my dad just chilling before the dog madness happened

I was a 17-year-old South African who had received a soccer scholarship to Lander University in the United States. The time had come for my last family vacation. My family rented a house on the beach, and uncles and aunts joined us for a week as they said goodbye to me before I left for the States.

It was a great sunny day. Many of the houses in South Africa at that time, especially the vacation homes near the beaches, had high fences, barbed wire, and often, guard dogs. The dogs would stay outside. They never entered the house. They were not pets. They were used just to protect the house and many of them were trained to kill.

The White Afrikan ~Who became an African-American~

My cousin Doug, who was around 11-12 at the time, and I were playing outside with a rugby ball. I kicked the ball over the fence of the next yard. As I went to see where it landed, two massive Rottweilers, at least 120 pounds each, met me at the fence where a sign that said "Enter at Your Own Risk" hung.

As I turned to walk away, I looked back over my shoulder and saw one of the Rottweilers pick up the ball. He walked about 20 yards before dropping it. He then lay down on the ball and looked up at me, almost tauntingly saying, "Come and get it." Dejected, I walked into the house. The ball was brand new. My sister and her husband had bought it for me as a gift to bring to the States.

I said to my uncle Gary (the one who nearly killed me twice already), "Hey, the dog got the ball. We're not going to get it." I knew that making this announcement to him would be received as weakness. He looked me dead in the eyes and said, "You're a baby. I'll go get it for you."

As he walked out, he said, "Come with me. I'll show you how to get it." I started to follow behind him, thinking it wasn't such a great idea, but I kept walking anyway. Apparently, my dad had the same thought and he looked at me and said, "Don't go." I said, "Dad, I'll be fine."

We walked out of the house and into the next yard. He opened the gate and walked directly towards the rugby ball. One of the dogs came at him full speed. Uncle Gary stared it right in the eyes and said, "Sit." The dog sat. He looked back at me and said, "Yeah, you're a baby."

He started walking toward the second dog. As he leaned down to pick up the rugby ball, I heard a very, very loud growl. The dog lurched forward, grabbed his arm, and started chewing on it like it was a rubber toy. While he was fighting that dog, the first one who had been sitting turned around and began biting him on the back of the leg. The attack was on, one dog behind him, one dog in front of him.

Somewhat aggressively, he yelled out, "Come and help me!" I ran straight past him and picked up the ball, because that was the mission. He may have failed, but I wasn't going to. As I ran back, I threw the ball over the fence to my cousin.

I looked back towards my uncle and noticed that he was concentrating on the dog that had bitten him from behind, in his hamstring. As this was happening, the other dog leaned back and launched itself at my uncle preparing for another attack. At that moment, my uncle turned around, the Rottweiler's open mouth catching him around the throat. He couldn't breathe.

The squeal that came out of him this time wasn't an angry one. It was more like, "I'm about to die, come and help!" I ran straight at my uncle to the dog biting him from behind and kicked it between the legs at least six times. Speed and power, I just kept thinking. It let go of my uncle, turned around, and then I kicked it in the head at least four or five times until it fell over.

Uncle Gary couldn't get the other dog off his throat. One of its teeth had pierced his hoodie around his neck and it was choking him. While it was still on his throat, he eventually pushed the dog over a hip-high wall onto its back near an in-ground pool. I ran and jumped at it, kicking it three or four times in the stomach. After that, my uncle picked the dog up and twisted its neck. I heard a crack. He threw it to the ground, looked at me, and said, "Let's get out of here."

As we ran to the gate, both dogs got up for a final chase. We closed the gate just in time. I looked at my uncle's arms. They had been shredded, pieces of meat hanging off them. The back of his leg was a mess with a chunk of flesh missing. When he looked up at me after surveying the damage to his body, I saw a two to three-inch hole in his throat, right near his jugular, and he was bleeding out of it.

Being the strong and crazy man he is, he walked back to the house and got some women's maxi pads, the kind they use for their periods, to use as makeshift bandages. He put one behind his leg, one on his throat, and three or four on his arm. My dad gave me his gun and told me to go kill the dogs. It wasn't safe, he had said. But as I was walking out, my uncle told me to leave them be. They had done their job.

We then took him to the hospital. He wasn't happy about that. The doctor said two more inches and the dog would have gotten the jugular and he would have died. He was stitched up with so many stitches that I lost count and to this day walks with a limp. We now call him Epol, which is a famous dog food that is sold in South Africa. That was one of the craziest days of my life.

Death by Chocolate...Almost

One night, I went out with my sister and her friends. It was nothing crazy, but we were late coming home. As was our habit, once we got into the house, we'd put the alarm on and walk down the hall to our rooms to go to bed. We'd see my dad's light on, say, "I'm home. I love you dad," and then tell him goodnight. No matter the time we arrived home, he would be in his room with the light on, praying that we'd be safe. It wasn't until we got back home that he'd turn it off and go to bed. This was a continuous occurrence for me. As I got older, I came home later, but that didn't change what he did.

On this particular night, I had a big ice cream in my hand and was halfway through it as I walked down the hall towards my room. It was tasting great. As I gazed into the room I realized my dad had to have fallen asleep during his prayer time. I must have startled him, because he jumped on the bed with his arms outstretched. It was kind of dark and I couldn't see, but I heard him say, "Put your hands up. Don't move, I'm going to shoot."

My dad's a funny guy. He's quite a character, actually, so I thought he was joking. I stepped towards him, and I said, "Dad, it's your son." He said, "I'm not going to say it again. Hands up, don't move, or else I'm going to shoot." That's when I got a little nervous. I'll be honest, I didn't feel like being shot in my own house. I saw him lying on the bed, with what looked like a gun in his hand, and I said, "Dad, my hands are up. It's me, your son."

Then he said, "Drop the weapon." Now the weapon he was talking about was an ice cream that I had in my hand, and I said, "Dad, it's your son. This is an ice cream." He said, "Drop the weapon." So I had to make a choice - get shot or drop a chocolate ice cream on his carpet. I went with the chocolate ice cream on the carpet.

As I dropped the ice cream and put my hands up, I said, "I've dropped the weapon. My hands are up. Don't shoot." He said, "Get on your knees." And as I was about to get onto my knees, my sister walked in, and said, "Hey dad, love you. I'm home." My Dad awoke out of his "trance," and said, "Okay, love you guys. Go to bed."

I was on my knees, then on my belly, lying right where I'd dropped the chocolate, recovering after almost having a heart attack. He turned his light off and it was time for me to go to bed. Just another day in the life of the white African.

The White Afrikan ~Who became an African-American~

Catching a Thief

<hr />

It was another beautiful summer in 1989 in Durban, South Africa. I spent most of my days on the beach hanging out with my buds. We'd hitchhike over there, spend the day playing rugby, soccer, surfing, body surfing, body boarding, or just chilling, and then hitchhike home.

That summer, the father of a friend of mine bought two Astro-NASA Spinning Circles, the ones you climb into and rotate around in to build your core. These machines were used by NASA to train astronauts to move when there's no gravity. They learn how to spin, rotate, and control their movements through this apparatus. My friend got me into it. I was doing it and it was great. Crowds would gather to watch me operate it. Then he asked me, "Hey, would you work for me?" I said, "Sure." People could pay five Rand to try it for five minutes. Most of the time I had to spin the bars for people as they didn't have the muscles in their core to do it. This will be a fun summer, I thought. I'll make some money, work on my core, meet some people, etc. I'll do it mid-morning, then take off and have the afternoon with my mates.

We did this for a couple of months that summer. I loved it. It was my number one summer. One day, there was a big commotion on the beachfront. This wasn't uncommon because there were a lot of vendors selling things. I heard people yelling, "Catch him, catch him! He's stolen some jewelry!" I looked down the boulevard to see a fellow running full speed in my direction holding what looked like chains in his hands. Two policemen were chasing him, but they weren't getting that close. So I thought, okay, let's help out. This wasn't a new thought. I had made citizen's arrests numerous times before.

As he was approaching, he took a turn and ran behind an area of bushes. I couldn't really see him but I knew he was back there. I told my mate that I was going to catch him. I took my money bag off and threw it to the ground. I had only my trunks on, no t-shirt, no shoes. I started chasing the guy at full speed. I could see him just a little through the bushes which were about at a medium height. He had crouched down under them. At what I thought was the right time, I dove over the bushes. As I did, he turned around and pulled out a knife. He was about to stab me when one of the two policemen, who had split up and gone another way, tackled him from the side. I was able to dive out of the way and avoid being stabbed, and then helped get the knife away from him. While the police put the handcuffs on, I was able to catch my breath and then helped put him in the back of the police car. They closed the door, said, "Thanks for your help. Enjoy the rest of your day," and that was that.

Another fun story in the life of the white African, a term I use only in retrospect now. I was one of course, but never actually realized it. I am proud to be an African. I am just a white one!

The White Afrikan ~Who became an African-American~

Fee or Flee

It was 1:00 or 2:00 in the morning and the phone rang. Now, when the phone rings at that time of the morning, you know it can't be good news. I overheard my dad say, "I'll be over there in a second."

I always slept with my door closed and two things under my bed - a knife and my baseball bat. My dad kicked the door open and said, "Listen, someone's attacking your aunt, we're leaving now. Get your knife and your bat." This was my aunt Fiona ("Fee"), mad uncle Gary's wife. I grabbed both and dad grabbed his two guns. We jumped in the car and drove very fast, through stop signs and red traffic lights. Instructions followed. "Listen, when we get there, you're not talking to anybody. Someone's trying to attack your aunt and get into her house. Your uncle's away on business. We're going to kill whoever we see. You get it?" he said. I was 14 years old and had just gotten a direct order from my dad. You didn't question it, you got your killing glasses on and got ready to go.

As we arrived at the house, we could hear the doorbell ringing. Someone was was either playing games or trying to get into the house, but they kept pushing it. My dad and I walked around outside the house to see if anybody was out there. He went one way and I went the other and we met in the middle of the house around the back. He nearly shot me because he thought I was the robber. Then we went inside the house and checked all through it. Nobody was there. It must have been someone playing games. I thought to myself, "Great, it's time to go." My aunt and her two kids were there and they were fine. As I was leaving my dad said, "Where do you think you're going?" He handed me his .38 Special and said, "You're sleeping here on the couch tonight. If anybody opens this door, don't ask questions, just shoot them." And then he left.

I lay down on their couch and put the gun underneath it. In three different dreams that night, I shot my dad, my aunt, my cousins, and myself. It was the longest night of my entire life. Nobody came to the house, and nobody entered the house, but I was ready if they did because that's what life was like in South Africa when I was growing up.

The next day, my mom picked me up, took the gun, dropped me off at school, and said, "Have a fun day!" Wow, what a crazy night and what a way to start a morning.

Provision for the White African –

The Trip that Changed My Life

My first big trip was a trip that would change my life forever.

After 30 years of teaching in the public school, my mom was given a golden handshake, that is, she was thanked by the government for her years of service, and left public school to begin teaching in the private sector. With my sister, Carryn ("Caz"), in college, and me, a junior in high school, my parents realized time was passing away. So with the money she'd earned from her job, they decided to take the whole family to America. This would be a goodbye of sorts as we were all beginning to go in different directions.

My sister Caz, and her husband-to-be, James, would be leaving South Africa to serve as missionaries with YWAM (Youth with a Mission). They would serve with them for over 15 years. And I didn't know it at the time, but after this trip, I'd be leaving for America on a soccer scholarship. I presumed I would live there for the rest of my life.

My oldest sister, Shelly, was nervous about traveling with epilepsy (a condition she had developed from a brain tumor she had when she was a young girl; it nearly took her life), and she had a steady boyfriend. She really didn't want to go on this trip and be away from him for too long, so she stayed behind.

So, my mom, my dad, Caz, and I went to America. One of the main purposes of the trip was to see my mom's brother, my uncle Trevor, and his family, who lived in Pittsburgh, Pennsylvania. They had come to South Africa once before to meet us, and we had called them every Christmas for as long as I could remember to wish them well.

We spent most of our trip with them. We rented an RV, drove down the east coast together, and saw various sites. We had a great time getting to know them and exploring the country. I had a major list of things I wanted to buy in America - a leather jacket, Ray-Bans, Nike shoes, a Nike shirt, Nike jacket, all the standard issue gear, classic Levis. Don't forget the Levis. I'd had a job before I left to raise the money for all these important things. I worked at a pizza place called Humperdinks (in my next book, there are a few funny stories about that place, like being punched in the face by the owner for being cheeky).

It was great family time, probably our best, minus Shelly, of course. We went to lots of famous spots, like New York where we went on a bus tour, and Disney World in Orlando. We did all the touristy stuff. That was the first time we'd actually been on an intercontinental plane trip. It was well worth the 20 hours in the plane. While we were there, I noticed that soccer was a big deal in America and started thinking about what it could look like for me to live there and play soccer, so we unofficially looked at a few colleges to get the lay of the land.

After we returned home from the States, I started the process to make my way back to America. This included playing soccer seriously again (I had taken a four-year break to pursue rugby at Glenwood High School, a top-10 rugby school in South Africa, where I played for the varsity team). Within the year, I had made my state team and was in the national tournament of U-19 soccer clubs. I also trained professionally with coach Gordon Igesund who became the coach for the South African National Team later on at Alberton Callies. I had an offer to play professional soccer, but decided not to, and switched my attention to playing soccer and studying in America after my amazing trip.

I also started preparing for the SATs and sent my resume to colleges in areas where the weather was warmer. It was the beginning of the rest of my life.

College Credit

I learned a major lesson in preparing for college. It became very clear that God had my back. The provision He showed me from the time I arrived in America, over the next four years as a college student, and then after that was unbelievable at times. God is a great provider and His timing is always perfect. That fact would set the course for the rest of my life.

I had been given almost a full scholarship. My parents paid more for airfare and new clothes than they paid for me to attend college for all four years – an amazing gift from God. When I arrived at the dorms, I learned I had four great suite mates I would live and connect with for a year. They made my transition very smooth and comfortable.

I remember arriving with little money in my bank account and not having a lot of access to the things I might have needed. I was away from home and understood that the exchange rate affected things. I tried my best to manage without having to ask my parents for more money as they had done so much for me. I looked for work, but as a foreigner you have limited options. You are not given a social security card right away, and you need this card to get a job. Then when you get it, it has a stamp on it saying work must be approved by the INS (Immigration and Naturalization Service), so it's hard to find employers who are willing to hire you under these circumstances. But God knew the score and provided a few jobs at just the right times with the right pay for the right needs. I got a few side jobs as a soccer coach and referee that were approved by the school. The extra money I earned kept me afloat.

But there were many occasions where the Lord simply provided for me. I remember that on my very first day of classes, I didn't have money for books. To get around this problem, I borrowed them or tried just to go without them. But at the beginning of one of my classes, the teacher said, "You have to have a book for this class. If you don't have one, you'll fail." He went on to say, "That being said, one of my past students has given me his old book and I have it right here. So what I'm going to do is take all your names, put them in a hat and then pull one out. It's the first day of class and you get a free book. We'll start the semester like this." I knew before he even pulled out the name that it was going to be mine because God had already shown me that He was a great provider. The teacher pulled my name and that book was mine. It's so easy to remember because I knew it was for me even before it happened.

Another time, I was going away on spring break with one of my friends, Ed. It was going to be for a full week and I was broke. I knew it would be hard to hang out with the guys with no money. I also didn't want to be the guy who was always in need. We went to a nightclub and were having a good time dancing. As I was dancing, I looked down at the floor and saw what looked like a small wad of $20s. I picked it up. It was $80. There were a couple of people around me dancing, and I was trying to be cool, so I was like, "Hey, did you drop your money?" And one of the girls was like, "Hey, get out of my face." So I said, "Okay, I'll get out of your face with this $80." That $80 carried me for the week.

There were also times when the crazy African would do a few dares to make some cash. The dares varied and they never worried me no matter what they were, unless they hurt someone or involved me getting arrested. Many were eating gross things, like crazy stuff mixed in a drink with hot sauce and whatever else. I would just plug my nose and down the cocktail. Other dares put me in danger, but I always bounced out of trouble and landed on my feet. There were a few classics. A friend of mine dipped tobacco. After a few weeks, the Dr. Pepper bottle he had saved to spit in was about half full. My roommate said he would give me $10 to gargle with it for 20 seconds. No worries for me. I dropped that bad boy in my throat, gargled for 20 seconds, witnessed most of my roommates throw up, and grabbed my $10. Sometimes you just need to go with it.

It was story after story of how God provided for me in my day-to-day. Friends on my team would be like, "Hey man, I bought a pair of shoes and got a free pair" (buy one, get one free, never heard of anything like this in Africa). One of my friends said that to me and gave me the extra pair. Another guy said to me, "Hey, I got a brand new watch, but they gave me another one in a different color. You want it?" My second year in college, the school gave me a scholarship for a leadership program I never even applied for. It gave me extra money when I was away from home.

So it was truly an amazing time for me. I had very little, but in story after story, God showed up and provided what I needed and what was best for me. I was never in want. Those were great times, great years.

Par for the Course

———◆———

As I've said, God's provision for me in college continued over and over, and into my senior year. It was time to get an internship and I looked around and found a place in Greenwood, South Carolina, the town I lived in, near Lander University. There was a company called Warner-Lambert that made toothpaste for big brands like Colgate. They had an international office in this small town and I applied for one of the two available internships. I got the job along with one other guy, each of us with a different skill set.

I met my boss, Tina, on day one when I arrived. She was probably about 45 years old and just trying to perform well in her job and grow in her role at the company. She was the one in charge of hiring the interns. The goal with this program was to utilize the younger viewpoint of college students to help bring fresh ideas to the company. One of her main jobs was to build relationships with clients that had ownership in the company, many of whom were international customers. The spring I arrived, she was preparing to host all these international customers for a weekend. This would include a day at the Masters, one of the four major championships in golf.

One of my jobs was to help with logistics for the guests, like getting them from the airport to the hotel, then to the Masters and back the next day for the party that night. It was an amazing opportunity for me to put into practice what I had learned with the marketing degree I was working on and see how it actually fit in the business world.

The first few days at my job, I was just getting a feel for how things worked. Tina said to me, "Craig, you and the other fellow, I forget his name now, will be doing all this work, but you won't be allowed to come to the event." From the beginning, that was fine with me. I never had an issue with that. This was part of my internship and it was just a great experience. I went to work every day and worked hard managing all the details - finding out how to pick up the guests in the limos, organizing their stay at the hotel, preparing packages they would get when they arrived, helped organize the tickets for the golf course, and then helped with the party and entertainment for Saturday night.

I remember a couple of weeks in, a fellow on a phone call walked past me. It sounded like he was speaking Afrikaans, the language that I'd learned in South Africa. I stuck my head out and yelled back to him, "Yo yo, what's up, player?" And he carried on walking, raised his hand, and waved. I turned to my boss and was like, "Oh, who's that guy?" And she said, "Well, he actually runs the whole show." It was kind of funny that one of my first interactions with the boss was me thinking this man was a fellow South African. He was actually from Holland, but I realized that our language had been intertwined.

Anyway, a couple of days before the kickoff of this amazing event, Tina came to me and said, "Craig, you've done such a great job. I want you to be at the event all three days." This kind of blew my mind and I was like, "Wow, this is spectacular." And then she said, "I'm not asking the other fellow, I'm only asking you," which was also spectacular.

So I ended up wining and dining some of the big name people from all around the world, being available for them, and driving them down to the Masters, etc. Then Tina had said to me, "Hey listen, I don't think you're going to get into the tournament and actually walk the course with the rest of us." I was fine with that. About halfway through the game, she came to me and said, "Hey, a couple of the clients want you to walk the rest of the course. Would you be okay with that?" I was pumped. I said yes, that it would be spectacular, and jumped in a golf cart, got into the facility, and then walked the course with a couple of these CEOs.

As I was walking around, I actually saw Ernie Els on the 16th hole, I think it was. Because he's a famous golfer from South Africa, I yelled to him in Afrikaans. "Hey, Ernie, hope you do well. Have a great day." Well, he stopped and said to me, "Hey, I'm finishing this hole, I'd love to see you at the next." I was expected to wait while he hit the ball. After that, he called me over and I walked two holes with him. He just spoke to me and encouraged me. He's an amazing man and a huge celebrity. It was great just to be around a fellow South African and be able to get some wisdom and advice from a very famous man. When I returned, the fellows I was walking with were highly impressed. It made their day. I went back to Tina and told her the whole story. She was clearly overwhelmed and I ended up staying to finish the event that evening.

The internship was great, and a great opportunity. It was another example of God's graciousness to me, of just giving me favor and access to things and people that I didn't deserve. As it turns out, much of my life would follow this pattern.

A Little Help from My Friends

As my college years were coming to a close, I realized how thankful I was for my roommates. The first year, my roommate was Todd, a fellow from New Orleans. My other suite mates were Ed and Jean, both from Florida. These young guys helped me and looked after me and introduced me to life in the States my first year. All of them were very kind and hospitable. As a foreigner, I didn't have a place to go when the holidays and breaks came. During every one of these major times, like Christmas and New Year's, Easter, and spring and summer break, when you can't imagine being on your own, they never hesitated to invite me to their place to spend that time with them and their families. The following year I lived with Jimmy, Mario, and Keith. And again, these three fellows opened up their friendship, their homes, and their families to me. Year after year, this had an impact on my life.

As I reflect on it now, I know I was thankful, but I wish I had done more to show it at the time. My friends really took care of me, drove me places, fed me, paid for my gas and other expenses. There have been times since then that I've chatted with them or sent an email just to thank them for the impact they had on my life. I am so very thankful for my friends.

My final experience with this generosity during those years was when my roommate Jim offered for me to stay at his parents' house after I graduated. I thought I had one more year left on my visa. Jim was finishing his last year of college and lived on campus. He was on a five-year plan. I actually ended up staying with his parents for six months and they introduced me to the club and town soccer world. Carol was the administrator of St.Giles soccer club, and through her, I got my first youth soccer coaching job in South Carolina with a team called Die Span (The Team), which is an Afrikaans name. When I was with them, we actually won a state championship. At the same time, I was also the goalkeeper coach for St. Giles, soccer club. That summer, I worked there full-time in the afternoons but also worked mornings as a forklift driver in a warehouse to make more money and keep me out of trouble.

Jim's parents, Frank and Carol, looked after me and made me part of their family. It was during this time that I fell in love with soccer in a different way, as a coach, and saw that I could earn a living from it. I began studying to earn a degree in sports management and coaching, but then realized that I could do this in a hands-on way without the degree.

My friendships were a major factor in keeping me in the States. Without them, I don't know where I would have been. They changed my life. And once again, I had seen God's provision as He stabilized my exit from college and I entered into a new phase of life where soccer would be more than a passion. It would become my profession.

The White Afrikan ~Who became an African-American~

The Passions of the White African – Soccer and Faith

If you know me, you know that I'm a very passionate person. It's just part of who I am. In my 20s, the two areas of my life that I was most passionate about were my faith and soccer. The two things I loved most would intertwine during those years, and that fact would change the course of my life forever.

It was late November 1998, and I was still living with Jim's parents in South Carolina. I started to search for a full-time coaching position with an organization that would provide me with a work visa. Because St.Giles was a young club, this was not something they could do. I went online and typed in "soccer job with visas." A company called Soccer Extreme in Connecticut came up. They had a 1-800 number (the phone call was free), so I called. John, the owner, was interested in having me interview for the job, so I flew up and spent two days in Connecticut. He offered me the job and said all I had to do was get my visa changed to a work visa as I was no longer a student. There's a window of time to apply for a student visa to directly transfer to a working visa, but I had missed it. The job with Soccer Extreme was guaranteed, but I had to have the visa.

After speaking to my lawyer, I found out on Christmas Eve that I had been illegal in America for the six months since graduation without knowing it. The lawyer's advise to me was to go home as soon as I could and apply for a tourist visa. In order for my passion about soccer to become a reality, my other passion, faith, would have to kick in over the next nine months.

I flew home to South Africa, and as quickly as I could, went to the U.S. Embassy to see if I could get a tourist visa to get back to America. I could then transfer the tourist visa to a working visa and begin my job at Soccer Extreme. The crazy thing was, if they checked my passport and visa, they would have discovered that I'd been living in America illegally. When I arrived at the embassy, I informed the lady that I wanted to do three things with my tourist visa. I wanted to see my roommate graduate, attend another roommate's wedding, and I wanted to travel. The woman behind the counter was very angry and rude and told me that I could have attended any number of graduations and weddings during the last five years I'd been in the States. She wasn't interested in me or my particular situation and stamped my visa "CANCELLED WITHOUT PREJUDICE," which means I couldn't return to the U.S.

At the time this was a major blow, but eventually, I came to realize that staying in South Africa would propel me into the next chapter of my life. This woman was just part of my story. She had done the best thing for me. They updated my status in their computer system and I was able to apply for a new passport. I had not been considered illegal, nor had broken any rules in the eyes of the law. I then had to go through the process of applying for a temporary work visa granted to people with special skills that allow them to work at a specific job that can't otherwise be filled by a domestic employee. This was not an easy task for a soccer guy. The "special skills" usually applied to people like lawyers, doctors, and certain other professions; they denied most applicants from Africa and other places who just wanted to leave their own countries. John would hold the job for me. It was a position he really needed to fill as his company was growing, but neither of us knew then it would take nearly a year for me to get back to the States.

My dad allowed me to stay at the house for free and I worked at the church as a youth pastor for the next nine months. One of my main jobs was to help out at an orphanage and get the kids from the orphanage to the church. My faith grew tremendously during that time as my soccer dream faded. Then all of a sudden, God changed the plan. My visa arrived unexpectedly and I

The White Afrikan ~Who became an African-American~

returned to the States to fulfill my dream.

I Thought it Was Soccer

I returned to the U.S. in September 1999 ready to begin my job at Soccer Extreme and pursue the sport full time. Soccer was my passion. It was a huge part of my life and identity, and was now my profession as well. But, it was also my passion to love Jesus. I was just wondering how I would combine these two things.

The soccer world was full of amazing young men, most of them wild and crazy. Many of them didn't know God and didn't care to. But I was thankful enough to be in a position as an employee where I could share my faith in practical and real ways. I learned how to evangelize, to tell people about God without making them feeling guilty or pressured. This was a breeding ground for me to learn how to manage a business centered around a passion, and be a mentor at the same time.

A cool thing happened at the office one day. It was time to renew the visas for the foreign guys who worked for me. I told all the fellows to bring their passports in as they all had to be submitted. No passport, no work. All the guys brought them in except for one, Kevin. I looked out the office window and saw that Kevin had completely dismantled his car. Everything that had been in it was outside of it. After a good while, he came up to the office and said, "Boss I can't find my passport." He said he had had it when he left home, but that it was now not in the car. "Well, ok bro, where is it?" I said. At that moment, I clearly heard God say it was in the car, so I mentioned this to Kevin. He looked at me, pointed to the mess outside the car, and said, "If it's in that car, I will go to church with you Sunday. This was a huge thing for him to say because he was a wild man. Kevin going to church would be just as likely to happen as the walls of the office falling down. I blurted out, "Good, because it's under the seat of your car. The Lord showed me that." He laughed and said he knew it wasn't there because he'd looked there 10 times already. So there I was, all up under the car seat digging around with him laughing, but there was no passport there, just his soccer boots. I start praying, "Lord, what's up?" He said, "Look in his boots." I pulled out the boots, and rolled up in the toe was his passport. It blew Kevin's mind, and he did go to church with me one time a few months later. Fast forward six years, after walking with Kev through some tough stuff in his life. He surrendered his life to Jesus, and he is one of my good mates today. This is one of the many powerful stories God has allowed me to to be part of.

And so it was that I began to realize that there was more to my life than soccer. The Lord was using my love of the game to connect and establish amazing relationships with people who didn't know Jesus. I tried not to be offended by their decisions and lifestyles. They didn't always align with mine. But through my passion for the game, God was preparing me for my other passion, the one that was most important in my life, Jesus. The soccer world had been good to me. When John first hired me, the only thing I asked for in my bare bones contract was the possibility of obtaining a green card which would allow me to stay in America. But every year with Soccer Extreme, my contract grew, and within five years I was actually running the company. We had 50 employees and were worth about $2 million. Again, it was clear God had provided for me and given me favor. He put me in a good-paying job in a position of authority, all because of my passion for soccer.

I was dealing with some pretty hard stuff at the time, but God would bring a group of people into my life who introduced me to Sanctuary, a ministry at a church in Fairfield, Connecticut (more about this in the next chapter). One of these men stands out to me, Kevin Butterfield. Once I joined this community, things began to change significantly. Right before my eyes, my passion for soccer was diminishing and my passion for Jesus was

The White Afrikan ~Who became an African-American~

increasing and I realized He was leading me into ministry.

The Power of Sanctuary

A small Bible study for young adults was being held on Wednesdays at the church I went to in Cheshire, Connecticut. A few of us saw an advertisement for free coffee on Sunday nights at a place called Sanctuary at another church after the evening service. We had been looking for opportunities to meet other Christians. So about 12-15 of us from the church in Cheshire went to this church in Fairfield and discovered there were another 150-250 people our age, young adults ages 20-35, who obviously loved coffee too. We started attending there as a group, and started doing life together. We really enjoyed being part of this big community.

The fellow who ran it, this guy by the name of Kevin Butterfield, took me out for lunch to get to know me better. He wanted to know how I was pursuing God in my life and where I saw my future heading. At that time, I had been working through some difficult things. He asked me if I would be open or interested in helping him with Sanctuary, which I was. I was very

71

excited. A couple of months later, in addition to my full-time soccer coaching job, I took a part-time job with the church as the director of Sanctuary and began helping Kevin navigate and develop this community.

This large group regularly met on Sunday evenings. Some people attended other churches in the morning and then came to the evening service and some people only attended the evening service. We created community groups. We created sporting events and social events and made some really good friends. Some came in and made it their home. And actually, that's where I got to know my wife, Karly. I met her at the church in Cheshire, but got to know her better and outside the church during this time. Finding my wife there solidified for me that ministry was the next phase of my life.

I first went to Sanctuary just looking to be part of a community, but it changed my life. It has created a group of friends that I still have and know well. I found my wife there, and my call to ministry. I ended up working at Sanctuary for seven years with Kevin, and actually, that's where I started investigating a part of my life that I never knew was there. Well, I knew it was there, but I hadn't really explored it. I knew about God the Father, a loving father who sent His son to die for me, and I knew He watched over me. I understood and really loved Jesus, this man who died and sacrificed His life to give me life.

But I knew very little about the Holy Spirit, and that was the secret sauce.

So Kevin and I investigated more of what this Holy Spirit is about, and that's what changed my life and ministry. I started being taught by men like David Wagner and Jan Nel. These men spoke to me prophetically and spoke words of encouragement and knowledge into me. They taught me to tune my ear to the Spirit. They taught me to listen on behalf of others, and on behalf of God, and my eyes were opened to a broken world that needs the voice of the Savior and the still voice of the Holy Spirit. I matured in listening to the Spirit and learned how He can infiltrate, as crazy and weird as that sounds, every part of my being in my call to love and help anyone I come in contact with.

Living a life like Jesus - mingling, interacting, being around anybody from any background, any lifestyle, any circumstance - this, I learned, was my call - to love them like the Father does and then listen and discern the sensitivity of the Spirit to know what the Father would say to His son or daughter.

That was a powerful time in my life. I saw some great miracles and great movements of God. Sanctuary was, well, a sanctuary for me, a refuge, a place that changed my life. It gave me direction, and through Christ, some purpose, and prepared me for the next phase of my life when I would marry Karly, have kids, and move into ministry together. That would be a game changer.

Make Your Move

It was time to make a move. I was working at Sanctuary, which was supposed to be a part-time commitment, but I was working much more than that by my own choice. I was still running Soccer Extreme too. I had married Karly, the love of my life, whom I had met at church while helping with the middle school youth group. I had convinced her to work for me at Soccer Extreme as our administrative assistant. We worked together for two years, and I believe that if you can work with the person you're dating and still love her or him, that's a good sign. We got married in Lakeville, Connecticut on June 13, 2004, in the Berkshire Mountains. It was a beautiful day with family and friends celebrating our love for each other.

By this time, Karly and I were considering having a third child. I realized it wasn't sustainable to continue living the way I was living. Life was crazy busy. At the time, Kevin Butterfield answered a call to ministry in Australia, and asked if I was interested in taking over Sanctuary. I knew that I was being called into ministry. I just didn't know if this was the right time or place. I felt the Lord saying not to step in straightaway, that He had something else for me. So for the following year, I worked with Josh Feay to transition into the role with Sanctuary, and transitioned my family into the church in Fairfield which we began attending on Sunday mornings.

During that time, my soccer business had moved to another location which required me to drive past a church in Bethel. I had been doing this for a couple of weeks when I felt the Lord telling me to go in and pray in the prayer room. So I did. I would go in and pray and just ask the Lord what was next. I did this every week for many months. I knew I was being called to ministry, I just didn't know what that looked like. And my assumption was that I would be in some kind of soccer ministry where I'd use my passions for soccer and Jesus to change the world.

It was February 13th, and Karly's family wanted to go to a different church on Saturday evening of that week so that we could all spend Sunday together. This would be a place that was new to our family, but not entirely new to me as it was the same church I had been stopping in to pray every day. So we went to the service and the pastor spoke about hearing from God, a topic not many pastors were speaking about at the time, at least not in our area. At the time, my little Ayva was having nightmares and was very scared. The pastor and his team prayed over my daughter with such gentleness and kindness and love. The Spirit was moving. That night, Ayva experienced God's love and presence in a very powerful way (another story for another book). I knew the Lord was calling me to ministry in that space, so our family started attending this church.

I spoke to the pastors at our previous church in Fairfield, told them that we were moving to the Bethel area, and that we were feeling called to that church. I also shared that I'd been going to the prayer room every morning before work. It was clear that this was where the Lord had called me. But I still wasn't exactly sure what He wanted me to do. One thing had led to another. I had had an experience in the prayer room that I'd told a friend about. He told another friend, and then before I knew it, I was meeting with the church leadership who explained that they were looking for another campus in the town of Seymour. They asked if I'd be interested in being part of that team.

I was very interested. Karly was not. She was pregnant with Skye. She said to me, "You go ahead and launch that church, and when you finish, we'll come back to the mother ship." Halfway through the planning process for the church launch, the leader of that group asked me if I would speak to the senior pastor. I said, "Sure. He's a wise man. Why not? Let's have a chat." At the time, I interviewed with two Christian soccer companies. These were businesses that taught kids how to play soccer, but taught them about Jesus too. I was in the final stretch with each one, both of them pretty guaranteed, I was just waiting for the final nod. When I walked into the senior pastor's office, he blew my world and said, "Hey, we're looking for you to think about being the pastor of the Seymour campus. Would you consider that?"

Karly had driven with me to the meeting with the senior pastor, and on the way home asked, "Hey, what did you and the pastor speak about?" And I said, "He was wondering if I would be the campus pastor for the Valley." Straightaway, Karly said "No, we're not doing that." Normally that would get me fired up. I don't get excited about many things - what we do, where we go, where we live. When it came to spiritual things though, I was excitable, but I felt the Lord say, "Hey, just keep quiet." And I did. We drove the 40 minutes to get home, and just before we pulled into our house, Karly said, "Hey, do you think the "Jones'" would be interested in joining this ministry with us?" And being a wise man, or so I thought, I said, "Okay, before I answer that, is this a trick question where I begin to engage and you say to me, 'So it looks like you've made your mind up already.'" She said, "No. I've known that you were called to ministry. It just came sooner than I thought."

After much prayer and consideration, and even some prophetic words from friends, Karly and I knew that this was our next step. That year, I took the job as campus pastor in Seymour.

The White Afrikan ~Who became an African-American~

We made the move and the journey began.

The White Afrikan ~Who became an African-American~

The Plans of the White African – Ministry and Family

———◈———

It was clear that God had combined ministry and family into one. This was His plan. For the next few years, I got to see our family do ministry together with both individuals and other families.

Seymour is a blue collar town. It was very similar to where I grew up. As the campus pastor, I quickly engaged with the local store owners and other people, and the town itself. We met in a movie theater every Sunday. I got to know the local pizzeria and diner. That wasn't hard to do, as I love food. I spent time with the people on the street in and around Seymour where the church was located.

I met with the mayor once a month, asked him what his needs were, and how we could help him. I also met with people from the Culture and Arts Commission to find out what they needed and how we could help them. We became very involved in the community. There was a town event pretty much once a month. Whatever they were doing, we did it too. Valentine's Day, Halloween, Christmas, Easter, whatever the occasion, we joined in. The town would put on a fair or something and the church would have a booth. My family would participate in this as part of our ministry. We got to experience some amazing things, amazing stories, amazing miracles.

Seymour is a sports-oriented town, so we launched a soccer program called Champion Soccer Training. Karly helped me on an administrative level and my kids played in the program with me. More than 300 kids came through the program over a four-year period and about 30 kids surrendered their lives to Jesus. It made such an impact on some of the fathers that they started going to church. Crazy things were happening in the ministry at that time.

And then, God called me to be the family pastor at the Bethel campus of our church. From the beginning, I stepped into this role and tried to create a culture for our kids to know who they are in Christ and for their families to come alongside them as they become world-changers. We had four mantras: you were designed with value and worth, you were designed with a plan and purpose, we will always tell you that God loves you, and we will have fun together. This was the backbone of our family ministry as we sought to engage kids and their parents. We held a whole bunch of family activities. My favorite was the family fair which replaced Halloween because some people were scared of that word. I was not, but the name needed to be changed to accommodate the nervousness of some congregants in the church.

Here's another cool story. My daughter and I were waiting to get into the photo booth at the family fair. We had provided some fun things for the community to enjoy that day, and this booth was one of them. The fellow working the machine arrived late and there was already a line. He couldn't get it working, so I went up to him and said, "Hey, are we doing okay here? Everything all right?" He said, "No man, this machine isn't working." I said "Hey, how about I lay my hands on this machine and pray for it and we'll see if it starts working? Will you be cool with that?" He kind of shrugged his shoulders and said, "Yeah, whatever, bro." So I laid my hands on the machine, prayed over it, jumped in, and took the photos with my daughter. They came right out. The guy was blown away, he didn't know what to say. Afterwards, he came and spoke to me and thanked me for doing that. Within a period of time, he gave his life to Jesus because he had witnessed power he had never experienced before, and it changed his life.

The family ministry was a time for me to speak life into kids and parents. It also gave me an opportunity to understand my own family as it was growing, and to speak life into my kids and have them join me in ministry. Once again, we had witnessed some really cool things as we came alongside people and gave God the glory for what He was doing.When I entered into this position with my family, I never thought I would experience the love and power of Christ the way I did, but in His wisdom, God joined ministry and family together and the combination was amazing.

It's Not Magic

Billy's Story

Stories have the power to change us. This story has changed me and has awakened within me a greater faith in the power of prayer. It's a true story of Jesus encountering a boy and his father in the hospital ICU. This is OUR story, because God used our prayers to influence the outcome.

I was the campus pastor at our church's Valley location and had been a soccer pro for years, coaching a girls' all-star team. Gillian is one of the gifted 9-year-olds that I coached. On August 28, 2011, just after Hurricane Irene swept through the Northeast with 115 mph winds, I received a phone call. Gillian's dad was calling to let me know that she "might not be herself" at practice the next day. Her brother had been in an accident. When Gillian came to practice, she was completely shaken and lacked her usual self-confidence. As I approached her, she just broke down in tears. When her dad's fiancée picked her up from practice, I heard the whole story.

The day before, on the 28th, Gillian, her brother Billy, his stepbrother Seb, and the rest of their family went outside to survey the damage. The dad tested a tree swing in the yard to see whether or not it was safe for Billy to use. It looked good, so Billy was told he could swing on it. All was well until a horrific cracking sound sliced through the air. The tree holding Billy's swing had broken and began to fall. Billy jumped off the swing and ran to get out of harm's way, while his stepbother stood frozen in fear. His dad lunged toward him instinctively, moving him out of the way, but as he did, he saw that Billy had tripped over a root and fell. The whole family watched as the tree landed on Billy's head. His dad rushed towards him, and with adrenaline pumping, hoisted the 500-pound tree off his son's body. Wiping the blood from his small face, he looked to see if his son was breathing.

With the damage from the hurricane impacting the roads and making an ambulance's arrival difficult, the dad picked up his son's limp body and drove him through the post-storm disaster to New Milford Hospital. Billy was then taken by ambulance to The Maria Fareri Children's Hospital at Westchester Medical Center in New York and put in a medically induced coma in the ICU. He had three steel rods in his head to monitor his brain, and tubes coming out of his body to keep him alive. The doctors gave

Billy a 1% chance of survival, and very little hope for normal brain function.

As I listened in shock to the news, my own heart filled with love and urgency, and I decided to visit Billy in the hospital. There, I met Billy's dad, and asked if I could pray for Billy. His dad said, "I don't care, do whatever you have to do." With tear-filled eyes, I began to pray out loud to Jesus, that He would heal Billy and restore his life. During the prayer, Billy's toe moved. His dad responded excitedly, "He moved, keep doing your magic!" I assured him this was no magic, but that Jesus has the power to heal. During that time, the church staff joined me in praying for Billy using the emergency prayer email system we have in place to send out prayer updates.

Over the next four weeks, I visited Billy in the hospital at least once a week to pray for him. On several occasions, God would touch a part of Billy's body during prayer and his fingers would move. At one point, Billy even sat up, gave his dad a high five, and then lay back down. His dad kept shouting to me, "Do your magic, do your magic, it's working!" Again, I assured him that it was Jesus who had the power to heal, and that it wasn't magic. God moved in power as we cried out to Him in prayer over those weeks. After a few weeks in a coma, Billy woke up. His father called me crying.

Billy was then moved to Blythedale Children's Hospital, a specialty children's hospital in Valhalla, New York. It is the only independent children's hospital in New York State. The hospital is dedicated to the diagnosis, care, and rehabilitation of children with complex medical and rehabilitative needs. Billy spent a few more weeks there and I again visited him once a week and prayed for him. Billy was able to return to Connecticut after nearly six months. Today, he doesn't have a scratch on his head, and the doctors report that his brain function is completely normal . He is once again the talented athlete he was before his injury, and he's very happy to be alive.

The picture below shows Billy (left), on his first day back to school in January 2012.

I don't know why God doesn't always heal us when we pray to Him, but I know this - Jesus has the power to heal. This story compels me to keep on asking and believing through prayer that there are others Jesus wants to encounter with His healing power the way He encountered Billy.

The White Afrikan ~Who became an African-American~

I Hear You

---◆---

Cole's Story

Cole Thomas was born to Mark and Alison Hudak on March 10, 2012, after a picture-perfect pregnancy and delivery. Before being discharged from the hospital, Cole had failed a standard hearing screening in his right ear two times. Mark and Alison were instructed to set up an appointment with an ENT (ear, nose, and throat) doctor as soon as possible to screen him further.

Then, two weeks after birth, a very large lump appeared on the right side of Cole's neck. After taking him to the pediatrician, they learned that Cole had torticollis, an issue affecting the muscles in the neck which can occur due to the baby's position in the womb. They were told he would need to begin physical therapy immediately, but that over time the problem would correct itself.

Mark and Alison brought Cole to the ENT doctor where they screened his ears again. In his left ear, his hearing was perfect, but in his right ear, he couldn't hear anything. They were very upset by this news, but were reassured that the hearing loss would not affect his development or ability to talk because he had normal hearing in at least one ear. The doctor then directed them to Children's Hospital in Hartford, Connecticut for further treatment.

After hearing this news, Alison's younger sister, Lauren McGuigan, requested that the leaders of the church in Seymour lay hands on Cole and pray for healing in both his neck and ears. He was prayed over by the leaders that next Sunday after the service.

At Cole's first physical therapy session, Mark and Alison were told that he had a very "mild" case of torticollis and that it should resolve itself quickly. They went back for his second appointment two weeks later and were told that the torticollis had begun to heal so much that he did not have to come back. The therapists encouraged them to continue his stretching excercises at home and said that he would be just fine! What AWESOME news to hear!! They praised God for this and continued to stretch Cole's neck every day to complete the healing process.

They shared this great news with me and I shared it with the church family who continued to encourage them and pray for full healing in both his neck and ears.

The following week on May 10th, they went to the audiology department at Children's Hospital where both of Cole's ears were screened. Mark & Alison were hopeful that they'd receive a good report on his ears and neck based on what they had seen, felt, and experienced. They were shocked and devastated to learn the results of the test - that he had 40% PERMANENT hearing loss in BOTH of his ears, that this would affect his speech development, and that he would need the Birth-Three program three times a week and hearing aids. The doctors told them that the cochlear organ in each ear was not communicating sounds properly to Cole's brain and that that part of the inner ear CANNOT be fixed medically. Whether or not his hearing would worsen over time would be determined in the coming months and years. Mark & Alison were heartbroken to learn of this and immediately contacted their family and me. I invited them over for community group the following night, and once again, Cole was anointed with oil and prayed over for healing.

They then scheduled a follow-up appointment with a satellite office of Children's Hospital in Farmington where they were going to run the same tests they ran the week before to confirm the results found in Hartford. After this, the doctors would tell them how to proceed with treatment. Cole went to this appointment on May 18th while family, friends, strangers, and many members of our church family continued to pray for him. That morning, before they left the house, Alison prayed and felt God gently assure her that his name "Cole" was a part of the word "miracle,"or as I say, "miraCOLE." They continued to believe that Christ would heal Cole's ears.

The repeat testing began. 20 minutes into the four-hour test, the audiologist turned to them and with much happiness reported that Cole was showing that he had NORMAL hearing in his left ear! She couldn't explain why, but resumed the remainder of the test. When she finished several hours later, she told them she was confused by the results, but happy that Cole was somehow showing that he did NOT have permanent hearing loss in either ear, that he had normal hearing in his left ear, that both of his cochlear organs were working and communicating to the brain "beautifully," and that the hearing loss she was seeing in his right ear was a "conductive" hearing loss caused by an extremely narrow ear canal.

She concluded that in the 12 years she'd been running those tests, she had never seen follow-up test results that were so contradictory to the original results. She told Mark and Alison that based on the results that day, Cole would not suffer a developmental delay or have issues learning to speak. They were to bring him back in several months for another checkup, but at that time, there was no need to do anything else. Cole was FINE!! The icing on the cake was something that happened as the audiologist was leaving the room. She was several feet away from Cole, whose right ear was turned towards her. In a low voice, she said, "Bye Cole." He turned in her direction, looked right at her, and smiled! It was like he knew there was nothing to worry about, and through his smile, Christ showed them His grace. The three of them broke out into laughter as she said "Wow," and left the room.

*****Here's the part of the story that's crazy cool. The Sunday that Cole came to Seymour for prayer, the senior pastor at the main campus in Bethel came up with an idea. His video sermon encouraged congregants to pick up a key at the end of the service. Between all the campuses, a couple thousand keys were handed out. It was a powerful service as the keys symbolized the unlocking of the Holy Spirit in one's life, giving Him room to move. Karly was clearly moved by the message. She went forward, picked up her key, and put it in her pocket. She was crying so much (often a sign that the Spirit is moving in her), she did not even look at the key.

That night, after we prayed for Cole, Karly and I chatted in bed. We were so encouraged to see God act on our prayers and shrink the torticollis in front of our eyes, and feel Him move in that situation. We talked about the keys and how cool an idea it was. Karly had put hers on her nightstand after church. As she reached over to pick it up, she looked at it and gulped. "Look," she said. The key had "Cole" written on it.

We both were blown away that out of the thousands of keys given out, God would give us that key. We believe God was telling us to trust Him. It was as if He said, "I see you, and I want to show you how I am in the details." When we had heard the news that Cole's medical issue was still there after we prayed the first time, we continued to seek God. We asked Cole's parents to come back for more prayer. The story wasn't over at that point.

Our faith was high. Often, when God moves, the enemy tries to steal God's glory (the faith of his people), and will overplay his hand. We believe God went above and beyond, just to show us He was in it. We pressed in close to Him and saw Him at work, not just by healing the torticollis, but by giving Cole back his hearing. It was a joy and a privilege to see God move the way He did in this young man and his family.

Words and praise are not enough to convey the gratitude Mark and Alison feel toward their heavenly Father and their family and friends. The joy they've experienced because of what

He's done goes beyond the words of any story. God is worthy to be praised and Cole will live his life for Him sharing with others the wonders of His grace and mercy!!

It's a Cruise

My wife Karly listened to Adventures in Odyssey growing up whenever she took a road trip with her best friend's family and whenever she babysat for these three young boys. They would listen to an episode of this kids' radio program every night at bedtime. Karly knew our kids would love it. They were young at the time, only in preschool and in the early years of elementary school, but they were hooked! Daily, they would ask to listen to it. So we joined the AIO club that gave us access to an unlimited number of episodes for six months. We have since listened to over 800 episodes (we basically listened to 30 years' worth in 3 years)! We drive A LOT. Our commutes to school and church are both about 30 minutes, just enough time to listen to an episode. It was the first thing they'd ask for the minute we got in the car. Every day. Every time.

A few months after that, in November 2017, Karly saw that Focus on the Family was doing a cruise with AIO, and she thought, "Wow, this would be our kids' dream come true!" But seeing that I was is in full-time ministry as a family pastor, she knew we couldn't afford something this extravagant. She asked me if I thought God would ever give us a gift like this? God has been so good to us. We've been given some amazing gifts from different people on our life journey, but nothing like a "real" vacation like this. Anyway, I believe God can do anything, and so I suggested she pray about it and also reach out to Focus to see if they offer scholarships for families in full-time ministry. Karly reached out, and understandably, was told they do not offer scholarships. I was also told that there were no "family rooms" left and that we'd actually need to book two rooms, which tacked a few more thousand dollars on to the price tag. She asked if there was a waiting list, which there was, and was told we could be put on it, but that there were quite a few people already in front of us. She came back to me and suggested we ask our kids to pray about the opportunity to take a cruise (we didn't tell them it would be an Adventures in Odyssey cruise). We knew we didn't have a penny to spare but we'd seen the Lord move on behalf of our family many times before. We also placed a fleece for that week, that is, we prayed the Lord would act on our request, and we would get the deposit for the trip.

Later that week, I met a friend for coffee. His wife had just had surgery and he asked our family to go over to pray for her.

We headed over and prayed for her from outside as she was too ill for us to go inside. As we were leaving, he handed me an envelope. When we got home, I saw that it was a check for the amount of the deposit needed for a family room. He just felt like the Lord wanted him to give us that gift. Wow! The only problem was that we were still on the waiting list. So now what? We continued to pray. A couple of days later, Focus on the Family emailed us. A family room had opened up! Karly had mixed emotions, a little bit of "wow," and a little bit hesitant. She knew that money could be used toward bills, but also knew we prayed specifically for this. She wasn't sure we should risk putting down a deposit we might lose, because at that point we didn't have the money for the remaining balance that would be due soon. I said, "Book it and trust the Lord will provide."

Within two weeks, we were given confirmation that the remaining money had been taken care of by someone else. How awesome is our God? We praise Him for the good gifts He gives. He takes care of our needs AND our desires. Amen.

A couple of months before the cruise, we realized that flights were very expensive and therefore figured that driving would be our only option. We live in Connecticut and this would require driving to Florida. We drive SO much, (which is both good and bad, good because it gives us time to listen to Odyssey!), that Karly felt this long drive might put us over the edge. One day, our kids asked us if we could please fly because they thought the drive would be too long. Karly told them that financially it wasn't possible, but that they could definitely pray about it. Meanwhile, Karly sent me a screenshot of what it would cost for airline tickets ($1,150 for our family). Prices were soaring due to the Thanksgiving holiday right around the corner. That afternoon, only a few hours later, I came home from work to find I had received my paycheck from a coaching job I have on the side. I pulled out not one check, but two. The second one was a check for $1,000. Our friend told us to do something for the kids with the money. So, we were able to use it to purchase flights to Florida (our kids' first flight that they remember). GOD IS SO AMAZING!

A family photo on the cruise ship (front, left to right, Ayva, Skye, Keane, back, Karly and me)

Ayva and Skye's late-night swim

Left to right, Ayva, Keane, Jess Harnel, the voice of Wooton Basset on Adventures in Odyssey, Katie Leigh, the voice of Connie Kendal, and Skye

The White Afrikan ~Who became an African-American~

The Father's House

When I went into ministry, it became apparent that we would not be able to afford the house we had bought a few years before. We thought this would be the home we'd raise our children in, but that was before I took a job at a local church. After a few long years of trying to sell it, the process ended in a short sale. The bank sued us for a portion of what we owed on it. It turns out that paying your mortgage with a credit card for two years to honor your commitment to pay your bills, leaves one with the feeling that you did the best you could, but also leaves one with a tremendous amount of debt.

Although waiting for the house to sell was frustrating, we saw again how the Lord's timing is perfect. The month before our sale went through, Karly's parents temporarily moved out of their house and offered it to our family. It's the house Karly grew up in and it held many good memories for her. Our kids were able to make some memories of their own too.

The return of Karly's parents had been up in the air, so we planned out our lives one school year at a time. One snowy day in February, school had been cancelled and Karly was home with the kids. Karly's mom called, and with her on speaker phone, announced that they'd be coming back at the end of that school year. This caused a little bit of a panic as it also lined up with the departure for my seven-week sabbatical. Our oldest daughter, Ayva, overheard Karly's mom and started crying. She said, "Mommy, where will we live? Where will we go to school?" Karly did her best to reassure her, but texted a friend with the very same questions.

Later that evening at the dinner table, I spoke to the kids about my brilliant idea to apply for scholarships for the next year to the school they were attending, and find a cheap rent somewhere. While it sounded like a reasonable plan, Ayva still wasn't happy. She said, "Can we please pray about this?" Oh yes, of course, let's pray, (ideally, I would have led the conversation this way...sometimes, kids can humble you). We went around the table and prayed for wisdom and provision. Five minutes later, Karly's phone chimed.

Her friend texted her saying, "Hey do you know that family that's moving to Australia? Maybe they need a house-sitter." Karly didn't know the family, but when she read me the text, I knew exactly who they were. I had met the husband a few years back at a Starbucks. I decided to send him an email asking if he remembered me and inquiring about the house. He replied yes, he had remembered me. We agreed to meet at that same Starbucks the following week.

He explained to me that his family had the opportunity to move to Australia for a year or two. It wasn't definite yet, but they were planning to visit there that April over spring break to help make a decision. He said that if they did move, we could stay in an extra home that was on their property while they were away.

I went home and told Karly this news and we prayed and waited expectantly for the Lord to move. For the 6 months prior to that, Karly had mentioned many times that it would be amazing for our family to be able to house sit for someone, but the reality of that actually happening seemed unlikely.

April came around and when the family returned from their trip to Australia, they contacted us saying they wanted us to come meet them and see the house. We planned to join them for lunch one Sunday after church. On the drive to their house, Karly said to the Lord, "I don't know what's going to happen here, but if you really love me, they're going to have a Nespresso machine." (When we retell the story now, she admits to how obnoxious that sounds.) When we walked in the house, one of the first things she saw was a Nespresso machine. I saw her eyes grow big. We had driven separately to their house that day, and so I was unaware of her conversation with the Lord.

We spent the afternoon with this amazing and generous family, and towards the end of our time spoke about us staying in their home. They graciously offered to leave everything in the home- all the furniture, beds, linens, kitchen pots and pans, utensils, etc. We only needed to bring our clothes. This was perfect, because that's all we had after living in Karly's parents' house for the last three years. The other incredible part is that while dreaming of our next house, Karly had created a sort of mental checklist of all the things she'd love to have. Everything on that list could be checked off! God is so good.

We told everyone we saw about the way the Lord had provided for our family, right down to the Nespresso machine. We spent the next two months packing and preparing for the move out of Karly's parents house, which happened in June on the same day that we began our sabbatical. After an amazing trip around the world, we landed back on U.S. soil and drove right to the new place we would call home for the next year and a half. When we walked in, we were overwhelmed with gratitude. The way the family had arranged for the home to be cleaned and decorated blessed our hearts. The way they thoughtfully had the fridge stocked with basic supplies so we could have coffee and breakfast the next morning blessed our tummies. The only thing missing was the Nespresso machine. It was nowhere to be found.

We told everyone who came and sat at our table the story of God's goodness and faithfulness. Life is full of uncertainties, but God provided the answers in His timing, and our family's faith continued to grow. When we got to the part of the story about the Nespresso machine, many asked where it was. We would say (and truly believed), that we didn't know, but that it was too specific a thing for the story to be finished."

Months later, just before Christmas, a large box arrived in the mail. Karly tore open the box and immediately texted me. "You'll never believe it! Guess what just arrived in the mail?" it said. The family, to whom we had not told the story about the coffee machine out of concern that we'd appear ungrateful, sent us a brand new Nespresso machine, boxes of Nespresso coffee pods, and three bottles of honey! This would be a machine we wouldn't use just for coffee. Every morning, it would be a reminder of God's goodness to us.

"He brought us to this place and gave us this land flowing with milk and honey!" Deuteronomy 26:9

The Potential of the White African – Now What?

The big question I ask myself has always been, "Now what?" What is my potential, and what is my purpose, and what is it that the Lord is calling me to?

In this time of family ministry, one of the things that has been impressed upon me along the way is that people are in need of a savior, and a friend or community. More and more in my years as a family pastor, people ask me to talk with them about the brokenness in their lives - their pain, their past, their expectations of themselves or those that were placed on them, their future too. They may not know it but they are looking for truth, truth spoken into them and over them. They need to know that God loves them, that they are not alone, they have value and worth, and that God has a plan and purpose for them. The church is often a place full of people who already know God. This is great, but it's not necessarily the same thing as experiencing

God. And what about those who don't go to church?

I have created space for myself, for lack of a better word, to be a life coach, and I find time in my day to be available to meet with people who are in such a place as this, people who are looking for those things the world simply can't provide. Sometimes, I'm just a sounding board over a cup of coffee. Some weeks, I meet with people three to four times, even six to eight times. Each situation is different and each person is different. But I have found beauty in these conversations. You may wonder how they find me. In various ways actually, often a friend has referred a friend, or my wife has found people for me to meet with. Sometimes, someone calls the church. Other times, these conversations happen with friends I've made along my journey, many from my past and present soccer worlds. Many have even been random while I've been out somewhere drinking a cup of coffee (I really like coffee). People may ask a simple question, and then it begins.

The idea is just to keep myself open to see what the Lord is looking to do in my life, taking any potential that I have and giving it purpose in everything I do. This idea of a life coach infiltrates all areas of life, for all kinds of people, not choosing the rich or the poor, the lost or the confused, just anybody who might need to hear from someone who knows Jesus. By no means do I push an agenda or force Him down their throat, but when I have meetings with people, there are some things I'll say. It usually goes something like this. "Hey, I'm not here to change you. I heard you had a concern or some issues. I'd love to chat, love to help. Understand that my default is Jesus and the Bible. I understand that yours may not be. There may be times when we agree and times we disagree. I'm not here to change your mind or convince you to believe in what I believe. What I do know, is that when I leave my meeting with you, I'll return home to my beautiful wife and kids. I'll hang out with them, have dinner, have fun, close my eyes, and sleep. I'll hit the pillow and be assured that the morning will come and God's mercy is on me and I'll start another day. The reason I'm sitting with you is I understand that you're not in that same place. So if I can help you, great. If not, we'll move on and go our separate ways." And I ask God to bless the time we had in conversation.

The question is, "Now what?" What has the Lord called me to? What does He want of me? Is it more of this? These are dangerous, searching questions and ones only He can answer. I'm open and available to work in the church, with the church, in the world, with the world, but what I'll never give up, or ever reject, is the love and power and authority that comes from knowing Jesus Christ. He is a gift, both for us who already know Him, and for those who have yet to receive Him.

The White Afrikan ~Who became an African-American~

Made in the USA
Middletown, DE
31 December 2019